LUCAS

IN

BIRMINGHAM

Best wish
Gordon Brunt
18/9/07

LUCAS

IN
BIRMINGHAM

GORDON BUNCE

SUTTON PUBLISHING

Sutton Publishing Limited
Phoenix Mill · Thrupp · Stroud
Gloucestershire · GL5 2BU

First published 2003

Copyright © Gordon Bunce, 2003

Title page photograph: Joseph Lucas.

British Library Cataloguing in Publication Data
A catalogue record for this book is available from the
British Library.

ISBN 0-7509-3390-9

Typeset in 10.5/13.5 Photina.
Typesetting and origination by
Sutton Publishing Limited.
Printed and bound in England by
J.H. Haynes & Co. Ltd, Sparkford.

Between the two Great King Street factories, 1930s. The occasion is not known, but perhaps the workforce was assembling before a works outing: they look too smartly dressed to be leaving the factory at the end of the working day.

Contents

Introduction

Photography is but another form of journalism. It records without words a moment in time that will give account, backwards as history, forwards as the future. The idea of presenting the book in this form has long been a dream of mine. It has taken years to collect together the wealth of material contained within its pages.

I have written this book for all those who helped to make Lucas a great company – from senior engineers to those who worked in the various offices. The laboratory technicians, the skilled men responsible for all the fire and security arrangements – all crucial in ensuring the safe handling of the various volatile compounds used within a factory. The inspection departments, who make sure the products conform to the standards set out by the draughtsmen and women who interpret the customers' requirements. The many who work on machines, conveyors, lathes, presses and the intricate assembling and machining plants – people whose skills have perhaps not always been appreciated. Finally, the works engineers – responsible for overseeing and maintaining the whole works in order for them to function reliably day and night.

Many books have been written on the history of the Lucas company, but none concentrate on the Lucas employees. This photographic collection focuses on those who spent their working lives at Lucas, both in work and play. I hope to remind people of the Lucas Company and of the many individuals who have worked there over the years. In some cases, several generations of families: husbands, wives, sons and daughters.

Sadly, the company is no longer Joseph Lucas Ltd, having been sold off in various takeovers. First came Varity Lucas, then TRW and now the giant American Northrop Grumman Company. However, to me and many others it will always remain the Joseph Lucas Company – or, better still, 'Old Joe'.

My grateful thanks go to all who have helped make this book possible. I hope that the endeavour will prove to be worthwhile.

Gordon Bunce

Foreword

by Dr Carl Chinn

Joseph Lucas is one of the most important and inspiring figures in the history of Birmingham. He stands alongside the eighteenth-century princes of industry such as Henry Clay, the patentee of the making of papier-mâché; John Baskerville, who effected an entire revolution in the process of japanning and who devised an incomparable form of type; and John Taylor, the Brummagem button king whose outstanding success was regarded as crucial to the development of Birmingham in the mid-eighteenth century. These three heroes of the workshop were self-made men – as was Joseph Lucas.

A working man who came out of Carver Street, Joseph Lucas knew what it was to rough it. He had his time out of work and he went through a rough patch when he drank too much. But through hard collar, doggedness and determination, Joe built up a business selling paraffin. So well did he do that he began to merchandise hollow ware – buckets, shovels, scoops and the like. And then he made the big move of his life. He bought the rights to the manufacture of an oil lamp. Soon after he started production in Little King Street and he laid the foundations for a major international concern, one that brought prestige and vast employment to Birmingham.

That Joe Lucas and his son were able to expand so successfully owed much not only to their own ingenuity, drive and entrepreneurship but also to the skills, loyalty and graft of their workers. The recognition of the input and significance of the workers is what has driven Gordon Bunce to bring together the evocative photos in this book. A key figure in the firm himself, Gordon recognises that Lucas's was indeed an institution. An institution that was driven forward by its employees as much as by its owners and which belonged to the workers as much as it did to the shareholders.

I congratulate Gordon on his achievement. Brummies of all kinds feel a bond with Lucas and have been dismayed to see the great business broken up and its name all but thrust into history. Thanks to Gordon and his efforts, the name of Lucas will continue to have a power and a resonance through those who made it one of the greatest manufacturing firms in the world – its people.

Professor Carl Chinn MBE

CHAPTER ONE

Lucas Remembered

I t has been sixty years since I stood at the corner of Wheeler Street and Farm Street in Hockley, gazing in awe at the mammoth buildings across the road in Great King Street. The buildings belonged to the Joseph Lucas Company Ltd. I remember being fascinated by the gigantic blocks of bricks and mortar, the thousands of windows which appeared to me like eyes, all seemingly gazing at me – this was my first sighting of this famous company.

Why this particular factory had such an appeal to me it is difficult to define: perhaps the sheer size of it might have been a factor. It certainly stood head and shoulders above any other factories in the district.

The year was 1943 and Britain was still engaged in war with Germany, a fact which consumed everyone's daily lives. Lucas Great King Street was surrounded by countless back-to-back houses and their shared wash-houses. This landscape accommodated many of the people who worked in the Joseph Lucas Company.

Such was Hockley and Lozells at this time and yet people here were born, lived, worked and died having known nothing better. For some, their world extended no further than the huge factory which dominated the skyline.

I recall people rushing out of the factory during their breaktimes or at the end of their shifts, endeavouring to obtain some commodity of sorts. The duration of their breaks on a warm day would see workers in and around the doors, sitting on the pavements, no doubt swapping stories or just enjoying a brief lull in their working day.

I was born in 1932 in West Bromwich, when many were out of work and pawn shops were common. When my family came to live in Wheeler Street, Lozells, it marked to a certain extent an improvement in our quality of life. Such were the circumstances all those years ago.

Some commuted to work from the greener and more acceptable areas; new houses had been developed pre-war in Kingstanding, Great Barr and Sutton. During the war years few people had their own transport, but public transport then was better and more reliable than it is today. Many cycled several miles to work each day, and the companies for which they worked provided bike sheds. Before the 1950s there was no great need for the large expanses of car parks that we see today, nor for the pavement car parking that now blights almost every street scene.

Early twentieth-century transport in several different guises.

It is difficult to see how people could escape from such a working environment – but they did. Many who grew up in this area became famous names in politics, sport and commerce. Perhaps the best known of these was Denis Howell, always to be known as Britain's first Minister for Sport, who served for thirty-five years as a Labour MP. He hailed from Guildford Street in Lozells, and then moved to Clifford Street. His house was close to our own in Wheeler Street and was also just a stone's throw from the Lucas factory. It is interesting to see how he described the entry leading to his own back-to-back house as a place of drudgery and despair, and the associated hardship of those not able to work. If one was fortunate enough to work for Joseph Lucas, however, at least there was pay and welfare.

Many of my family had worked for Joseph Lucas. My mother had been employed there and in her time had spoken to Harry Lucas himself – a very proud moment in her life. Other family members worked for the company as designers, planning heads and secretaries.

I joined Lucas in 1954, starting as a trainee in Gas Turbine, branch works no. 5 (BW5). Some years after completing my training I was promoted to Foreman in the Gas Turbine BW5 company. In 1964 I moved to BW3, which made starters and dynamos, and I was subsequently promoted once more to General Foreman, rising to Superintendent. This was followed by further promotion to Factory Manager. My working life with the company was to move me into different areas of manufacturing – lighting, alternators and drives. Finally, before my retirement, I became Executive Factory Manager, responsible for factories BW3, BW4 and Marshall Lake Road.

So the circle had been completed: the young lad standing on the corner of Wheeler Street and Farm Street, looking up at the mighty company called Joseph Lucas Ltd, had become a man who could look back from retirement at a long, successful and responsible career within that very company.

THE BUILDING BLOCKS OF SUCCESS

Over the many years in which I have collected Lucas-related material, it has come to my attention (with some sadness) that Joseph Lucas never saw how great the company he founded would become. Joseph was without doubt a visionary man who took opportunities where perhaps others never dared to tread.

It was the industrial boom of the late nineteenth century that gave him the means to move away from his occupation as a trader, trudging the streets of Birmingham selling his wares. Before his death in 1902 Joseph saw something of what he had strived for in the factory in Great King Street with his name over the door – a company then employing some 200 people.

While the company produced lamps for the growing safety bicycle market of the nineteenth century, they also made other items such as police lanterns and carriage lamps. The company's most famous lamp was the ship's Tom Bowling with its bicycle hub lamp – the 'King of the Road'. Lucas had started with oil lamps, then acetylene lamps, but its move into the motor car trade made it a major company and it became a main supplier over the following sixty years.

In 1897 the business had grown sufficiently for it to become a registered company. There is no doubt that being in the right place at the right time was also to play an important part for Lucas. The company that had begun with one man and his barrow now required head office organisation for its control.

Joseph had a very able son in Harry Lucas, and it was Harry who was to lead the company towards further expansion with the takeover of CAV and Rotex Ltd. Lucas became even more progressive when Harry was joined first by another son, Oliver, and later on by Peter Bennett. The takeover of CAV enabled Lucas to become involved in the manufacture of heavy-duty products, and this later became vital for aircraft industry requirements.

As a young employee in the 1950s, I found it interesting that Lucas had been involved in producing shells, bombs, aerial cameras and gun turrets during the Second World War, but the postwar period was a time of great advances for the company. After the war there were huge demands from both the private and commercial sectors for goods and Lucas was able to convert its wartime production to peacetime needs. The company had been involved in the production of the Frank Whittle jet engine, something I was to see on my visit to the Burnley works. By this time the company had taken over other big names like Girling brakes and hydraulics. Sadly, Oliver Lucas, the last major family member in the company, died in 1946. Lucas was subsequently controlled by its great chairman, Sir Bertram Waring.

Lucas had eleven factories in Birmingham and the Midlands: Great King Street, Shaftmoor Lane (with aerospace starters and lamps), Formans Road (plastics and

The first pedal-drive bicycles were made in 1839 and even today cycling remains a favourite pastime. The designs of the earliest bikes pose interesting questions such as how did anyone manage to ride them?

batteries), Girling (brakes and hydraulics) and Rocky Lane (lamps). In all the company employed 28,000 in Britain, 78,000 worldwide.

Lucas had come a long way since Joe walked the streets with his barrow, but alas this would all go: the factories would be pulled down or taken over. But they were – and are – still remembered with pride by those who worked there.

JOSEPH LUCAS – THE MAN

It is difficult to comprehend how one man could rise from the humble position of pushing a cart around the district of Hockley to become the creator of a company which at its peak employed nearly 80,000 people across the world. But Lucas was indeed an international company, and in Britain dominated the car industry for almost fifty years, as a supplier of parts required in the manufacture of vehicles both private and commercial.

Of course, while Joseph was the firm's creator, it was his son Harry and grandson Oliver, along with other illustrious names, who took the company to great heights perhaps never foreseen by the man himself. Unfortunately Joseph died suddenly in Naples on 27 December 1902 at the age of sixty-eight. He is buried at Moseley Parish Church.

Very little is known about the early life of Joseph Lucas. We know he was born on 12 April 1834 at Dingley's Buildings, Carver Street. His father was Benjamin Lucas whose occupation was listed as 'a plater of plated wares'.

His early life remains a blank in many respects, and it was his third wife Mary Anne who made known such information as we possess. She said that when he was a boy he attended a school run by a man called George Dawson, where he was taught to read and write. This was a big advantage in Victorian times, as few working people received any form of education and most children were likely to work from the age of about eight in order to procure extra income for their families.

Joseph Lucas with his first wife, Emily Stevens after their wedding at Edgbaston Parish Church in 1854.

It is said that Joseph Lucas was an apprentice in a company called H. & G.R. Elkington, which was part of the well-known firm of Delta Metal Ltd. Elkington's were an electro-plating company. As his father was employed in this business it is more than likely that Joseph was encouraged to do the same.

Birmingham has been the starting point and home for many world-famous engineers. This being so, it has flourished over the years and has grown into a major industrial centre. At the time Birmingham would have been the ideal place for a nineteenth-century go-getter like Joseph to make the most of his opportunities.

The pioneering days of Joseph Lucas began around the 1860s when he made his living selling wares on the streets. The business developed mainly from the sale of oil for lamps and he expanded into selling buckets and bowls. Joseph was not adverse to making money from those less fortunate and was known to lend money at interest, but by all accounts he did this in a very honest manner. By the late 1860s and early 1870 he had become a well-known tradesman and was already employing others in his business. *White's Directory* of 1873 lists him as a tin-plate work producer of ash-pans and also lamp-oil dealer. In 1882 his business was registered as Joseph Lucas & Son. By 1897 it had become a public company and Joseph Lucas Ltd was born. It was the simple lighting equipment for a Victorian bicycle that started it all, with the evolution of the motor car coming later and the aerospace industry a far off dream.

THE LUCAS FAMILY TREE

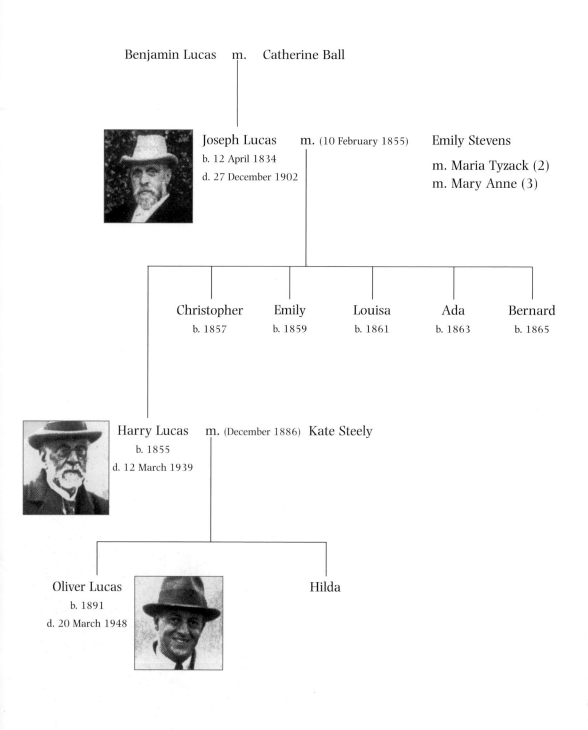

Benjamin Lucas   m.   Catherine Ball

Joseph Lucas   m. (10 February 1855)   Emily Stevens
b. 12 April 1834
d. 27 December 1902

m. Maria Tyzack (2)
m. Mary Anne (3)

Christopher	Emily	Louisa	Ada	Bernard
b. 1857	b. 1859	b. 1861	b. 1863	b. 1865

Harry Lucas   m. (December 1886) Kate Steely
b. 1855
d. 12 March 1939

Oliver Lucas   Hilda
b. 1891
d. 20 March 1948

CHAPTER TWO

The Factories

L ucas Great King Street was once defined as 'a huge rabbit warren' and with
good reason – as Lucas grew and grew over the years, so more buildings were
added on the site. Many of the original buildings were demolished to make way
for these new developments. The company was able to acquire extra ground on the
Black Patch recreation ground side of Farm Street which had at one time been the
area in which chemicals were stored. Owing to a serious fire there, that area
eventually became the new restaurant and theatre facilities.

Great King Street was in two parts: the manufacturing on one side of Little King
Street and the offices and administration facilities on the other. Buses would park and
wait for the workers to leave the factory at the end of their shifts, and hundreds of
employees would rush out to catch their buses home.

The only connection between the two buildings was an enclosed bridge with a
clock on the outside, through which workers could pass between the two parts of the
complex. At street level fork-lift trucks could make life somewhat hazardous as they
manoeuvred back and forth between the two buildings. I recall the French-designed
paternoster step-in lift, which was like a constantly moving staircase into which you
would step as it moved up and down.

Builders in Great King Street at the
start of the construction of the
Lucas group of factories in 1899.

While Great King Street was the main Lucas factory and the centre of administration, there were many other principal factories in Birmingham itself, and other stretching out as far as Cannock in the north and Solihull in the south. Those located in Birmingham itself included the Great Hampton Street and the Rocky Lane factories. Close by were Butlers and Formans Road, with the Shaftmoor Lane site and the Spring Road satellite factory forming part of the aerospace group, which also included York Road.

SHAFTMOOR LANE

The group of factories on the Shaftmoor Lane site which stretched across Spring Road consisted of BW3 (dynamo and starter), BW4 (lamp factory) and No. 5 Factory (gas turbine, which later became aerospace). The site employed in excess of 8,000 people and was a major employer in the district, with Formans Road battery factory and the Spring Road factories (a section of BW5) within walking distance.

The electrical company outlets appeared to work without undue problems with Gas Turbine on the same site and shared functions like the personnel department to avoid duplication.

The dynamo/starter factory BW3 had formerly been EIC Magnetos and was acquired by Lucas in about 1925. The lamp factory was purpose-built before the

Fox Hollies Road, *c.* 1925. This country lane ran close to Shaftmoor Lane and was eventually developed into a major section of dual carriageway.

Shaftmoor Lane, *c.* 1900. A one-time Lucas factory still stands in this area, but is sadly no longer part of the Lucas company.

Second World War in order to have a central lamp manufacturer. This pulled together all the lamps in the group.

The Gas Turbine factory was formerly used for other purposes and brought on to site during 1939/40. It was preconstructed, somewhat like a prefab house, and formed the Lucas Gas Turbine factory producing pump systems for aircraft engines. This grew and became a major part of the Lucas group, taking in more factories like Wolverhampton and York Road (formerly Velocettes Motor Bikes), Hall Green and converted to gas turbine production.

Shaftmoor Lane, Hall Green was a tranquil thoroughfare in the outer Birmingham area. It was to see change by 1927 and the gradual introduction of industry led to development and the quiet lane was all but lost forever. At the end of the nineteenth century grand houses were built at the upper end of Shaftmoor Lane for the middle-classes. Evidence of these still exists and with the increase in industry in the area, more and more houses were built. Today the area is busy and highly populated, and has many houses and factories.

Joseph Lucas Branch Works no. 3. Here we see the factory as it was in 1928. Note that BW4 had yet to be built.

The photograph below, dating from 1970, shows new stores extension, conference room facilities, bridging across to the main fire office of the factory today.

This page and opposite: BW4 Lamp Factory, Shaftmoor Lane, during the 1960s.

The packing department of BW4 Lamp factory during the 1970s.

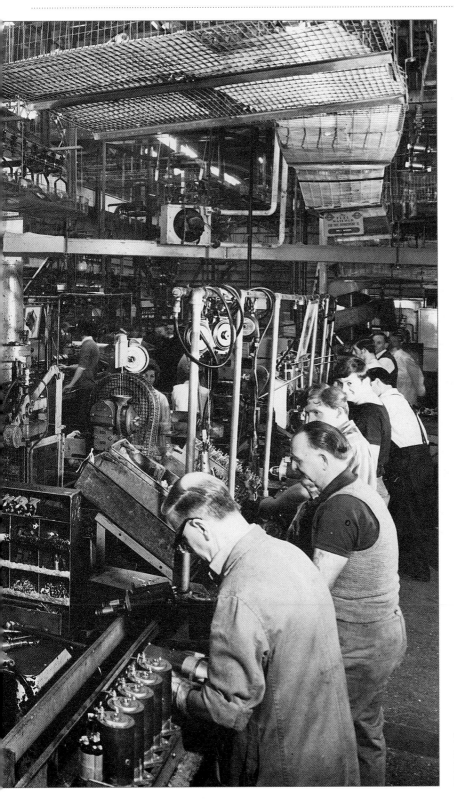

The starter motor assembly line at BW3 Shaftmoor Lane in the 1970s.

Lucas personnel and restaurant together with the theatre facilities was built in about 1970. The ornamental gardens replaced a Nissen hut building which was the Shaftmoor Lane branch of the British Legion.

An aerial view of the Shaftmoor Lane site. On the extreme left of the picture can be seen the arched roof of the British Legion building. In front of this area was Coronation gardens and tennis courts which were replaced by a large car park in the 1960s.

rom bicycles to Rolls-Royces – all contained
ucas parts.

Below: The Marshall Lake Road Alternator
factory was previously owned by BSA Guns.
t had been purpose-built in what was then a
ural part of south Birmingham. The cellars
of the factory were made to house testing
acilities for firing guns. The cellars remained
until bought out by Lucas who filled them in
llowing greater floor support for the heavy
machinery which was to be installed on the
ground floor.

is page and opposite: The alternator factory at Marshall Lake Road, Shirley, Solihull, in the 1970s.

Highly decorated scenes of Lucas, Great King Street. This was in aid of the Coronation of King George VI, 1937. Before Lucas built his factory there, Great King Street was described thus: 'rat infest shops, a jumble of terraced houses and shaded courts stood on the site, and there were two public houses, the Burbury Arm at the corner of Burbury Street and Farm Street, and the Brewers Arms in the lower part of Great King Street'.

CHAPTER THREE

Lucas People

In the early years Lucas had a Quaker attitude towards employees and their wellbeing. The company were considered a middle-of-the-road employer in respect of wages and salaries, but were highly regarded when it came to the welfare of its workers, regardless of their position in the organisation. This was the situation for almost the whole of its operating life. It was not until the 1960s that the situation began to change, when the unions, while acknowledging what the company did in terms of employee welfare, insisted that people were more interested in pay than facilities provided. Little by little a reduction occurred in company events, parties for workers' children, sports facilities, etc. Workers found themselves richer in pay, but this meant that the company were forced to seek ways of reducing their overheads and many employees found themselves being made redundant.

People ceased to be the first consideration. Factories began to close, workforces were being reduced in their thousands and a different outlook was being adopted – considered by many as a backward step. This was the beginning of the end and just a few years later the Lucas company would be history.

Machines and equipment are important, but so are the people who work them. However excellent the plant, it cannot function without people. Here are four Lucas girls at about the turn of the twentieth century.

Some of the brasscasters and the office girl, July 1895. Note the horse-cart on the extreme right which was at that time the company's transport.

A workshop in the Little King Street Works, June 1893.

Two views of assembly department BW3 in about 1935. Above is the starter assembly line, and below we see the horn assembly line. Note the wooden structure assembly benches and the very modern miss with knee-length boots.

Above: The press shop in BW4 lamp works, Shaftmoor Lane, *c.* 1937.

A Lucas pump (jet) rig team at BW5 Shaftmoor Lane in the 1970s. Eric Gillette (front, second from the left) was a popular team member.
The others are, left to right: Les Johnston, -?-, -?-, John ?, Bob Butler, Dave Sims, Dennis Godsel, -?-, John Carson and John Clarke.

achine shop BW3 photographed out of working hours in the late 1970s.

he BW3 starter assembly shop, *c.* 1970.

Above: M50 assembly shop at Shaftmoor Lane, 1970s.

Starter assembly BW3, 1970s.

Starter armature turning at BW3, 1973.

Coil winding section at BW3, *c.* 1970.

Above: Winding section BW3,
Shaftmoor Lane, 1969.

Peggy Stevens (foreground) and Linda
Perks (right) working on coil assembly
at BW3, 1969.

A group of assembly personnel on the RB310 regulator line, Great King Street, 1956.

A very nervous Sylvia Warton with the Duke of Edinburgh looking over her shoulder during a visit to Great King Street in 1956. Mr F. Gardner (director) is on the left of the picture.

happy group of ladies in the despatch
department, 1961.

Great King Street, RB310 regulator
adjustment, 1958.

group of Lucas ladies at Mere Green,
1976.

The opening of the new canteen at Marshall Lake Road.

Sir Bertram Waring was born on 12 June 1893. He was brought up in Manchester and was training to be an accountant at the time of the First World War. He joined the Lancashire Fusiliers, and was commissioned in the field to the rank of captain in the 29th Division at Gallipoli. Waring served for six years in the army. After he left he joined Joseph Lucas in 1922 at Great King Street. Some twenty-eight years later he had become company chairman. This was a position he held for eighteen years until he was seventy-six. In recognition of his unique service, the Lucas board elected him as the first honorary president of the company.

A.B. Waring (left) and Lord Bennett (right) accompany the Queen on her visit to Great King Street, November 1955.

THE FOREMAN'S OFFICE

This organised place of control was introduced by A.B. Waring in 1958. Every factory was provided with these offices, all set out in strict layouts providing graphs, charts and statistics to assist the foreman and provide information at a glance. Previously a foreman was expected to find a bench or some appropriate area in his department from which to control production.

Mr Waring had a model of the foreman's office made up in a glass case which was on permanent display at Great King Street.

Sir Bertram Waring is seen here welcoming the Prime Minister the Rt Hon Harold Wilson to Lucas in 1968.

Harold Wilson, whom I had the honour of welcoming to the Shaftmoor Lane factory in 1968.

JOSEPH LUCAS (ELECTRICAL) LTD

SHAFTMOOR LANE   BIRMINGHAM 28

TELEPHONE - SPRINGFIELD 3232 - TELEX No. 33-184   TELEGRAMS - LUSET   BHAM   TELEX

20th June 1968.

Dear Mr Bunce,

   I am sure that you were pleased and honoured to have been introduced to the Prime Minister on the occasion of his visit to our Factory on Friday last 14th June 1968.

   I want you to know that I feel the visit was a complete success, and I wish you to share this pleasure with me.

Yours sincerely,

R J Milburn.

Bob Milburn, factory manager at BW3 Shaftmoor Lane, explains operations to Harold Wilson. Cliff Jones, director of engineering, is looking towards the camera.

Frederick Jones was chauffeur to both Oliver Lucas and Sir Bertram Waring for forty years.

HILVER TRAINING SCHOOL

Harry Lucas House, opened after the Second World War played a major role in the administering of training. It began as 5 St Agnes Road and later grew to also include nos 7 and 9 as residential need increased. Later still a training complex of conference rooms and studios were built in the grounds.

Apart from ensuring the actual training staff would be there and things started on time, catering needs and general administration were also needed. I recall Christine Steven, a long-serving Lucas employee, who was the manager at Hilver. She was always approachable and acted in a firm but kindly manner, despite the heavy demands which were placed upon her.

The leadership course was a real pot boiler. It was run in a manner to create tension – which it did most effectively. The course quickly divided the men from the boys as pressure built up through the ten-day period. It was a tough course but so were many others run at Hilver. Should you be attending a course on management for foremen, you may have been in residence for several weeks over a period of six months.

David Fell was at one time the Group's Chief Fire and Security Officer and the responsibility for meeting such needs at Hilver (seen below) was under his management.

The gardens at Hilver House.

Christine Steven,
Hilver manager,
inspects food
preparation in the
kitchens, c. 1963.

The author as a young man (back row, fourth from left) at Hilver in about 1958.

Institution of Industrial Managers

This is to certify that

Gordon Thomas Bunce

has been admitted a

FELLOW

Given under the common seal of the Institution of Industrial Managers

In December 1990

MEMBER OF COUNCIL

SECRETARY

Lucas training was first class and encouraged by the company at every level. Time off was allowed to attend local technical colleges. Lucas apprentice training was rated as one of the finest in Britain.

MANAGING MANUFACTURING STRATEGICALLY

1   Introduction to Stage 3

The full programme for factory and manufacturing managers
is in four parts - the core parts being two, short, Hilver-
based seminars separated by a four week on-the-job period.
The detailed structure of the programme is set out in the
appendix; in summary the programme comprises:-

Stage 1   -   three-day Hilver seminar on
              'Manufacturing Strategy'.

Stage 2   -   four-week on-the-job period to
              test and apply analytical
              techniques introduced in
              stage 1.

Stage 3   -   two-day Hilver seminar which
              treats 'manufacturing in a
              business context'.

Stage 4   -   follow-up period: managers
              implement 'personal achievement
              plans' (with support from course
              tutors) and business executives
              examine the implications of
              organisational issues discussed
              with managers in stage 3.

This brochure presents the objectives and timetable for stage 3
and introduces proposals for the follow-up period.

An example of a training programme, *c*. 1980.

TRADES INSTRUCTION DEPARTMENT

The Trades Instruction Department, nicknamed the 'tiddlers', was set up in 1934. The apprentice agreement, a somewhat impressive presentation, was not issued lightly and those who speak of their days in the TID remember it was an honour – on a par with being knighted!

    Their apprenticeship also aimed to build character and to instil loyalty, discipline and fitness into its young people. Hard work made first-class skilled workers for the company and many went on to become managers later in their careers. Apprentices on this scheme worked 8½ hours a day in the week and 4½ on Saturdays – a total of 47 hours per week.

ROYAL SWEDISH EMBASSY SWEDISH DELEGATION 16th of May 1986 SAKAI PLANT KUBOTA, LTD.

Being sent to Japan for training on flexible production methods was a big thrill and very worthwhile. In 1986 I joined a Swedish delegation who were to undergo the same training. Conversation was difficult for me to follow at times, with most of it being in Swedish and Japanese!

CHAPTER FOUR

Lucas at War

At the outbreak of the Second World War the company switched all its facilities to the war effort. Production of jet engine fuel systems was transferred from CAV Acton to the Lucas gas turbine factory at Shaftmoor Lane in 1944. Rists Wire and Cables produced cables, plugs and sockets for Stirling bombers and Beaufighters along with telephone cable essential for communications in the field.

Some Lucas factories were bombed including Shaftmoor Lane, Great Hampton and Formans Road, which were all subject to aerial attacks by German bombers. In the years after the war German aerial photographs of the Birmingham area came to light on which Lucas factories were marked as targets. At BW3 the factory had been painted in a camouflage green and brown, but sadly it did nothing to confuse the bombers as the factory could be seen clearly from the skies.

The Lucas Home Guard 44th Battalion was led by Bertram Waring, who had served in Gallipoli during the First World War. The battalion formed a guard of honour during the royal visit to Great King Street of King George VI and Queen Elizabeth.

By the end of the war Lucas employed 40,000 people – a huge increase on the 28,000 it employed at the beginning of the conflict. During this time the majority of people employed by Lucas were women.

WE DEPEND ON YOU . . . .

Issued in the interests of Good Soldiering

JOSEPH LUCAS LTD. BIRMINGHAM 19

A Lucas wartime poster. (*Lucas at War*)

German wartime aerial photographs on which Lucas factories were marked as targets. (*Lucas at War*)

Below: King George VI and Queen Elizabeth are seen here with Lord Bennett and Bertram Waring visiting Great King Street in 1942. (*Lucas at War*)

A Lucas poster encouraging women to work at the factory to help with the war effort. (*Lucas at War*)

Lucas employees are seen here buying wartime bonds from commissionaire A.E. Maley. (*Lucas at War*)

bove: Gun turrets being manufactured at
ucas during the war. (*Lucas at War*)

More gun turrets nearing completion at
ne of the Birmingham Lucas factories.
A City at War, Birmingham 1939–45,
Birmingham Museums & Art Gallery, 1985)

" For King and Country — for Dear Life — for Freedom of Mankind."

JOSEPH LUCAS LTD.

This is to certify that

ERNEST THOMAS HICKERTON.

WAS EMPLOYED AT THE

GREAT KING STREET   **Factory**   FROM:– 8.9.41.
                                            TO:– 8.12.45.

IN THE PRODUCTION OF VITAL WAR WEAPONS & EQUIPMENT

FOR THE

ROYAL NAVY · THE ARMY · THE R·A·F
& SO PLAYED A FULL PART IN HELPING
OUR ARMED FORCES TO VICTORY

A certificate presented to Lucas employee Ernest Hickerton in recognition of his employment in 'the production of vital war & weapons equipment', between 1941 and 1945.

CHAPTER FIVE

Lucas at Play

The social life at Lucas knew no bounds. Almost every sport and pastime was catered for – football, swimming, motoring, dancing, caravanning – the list was endless. Many Lucas personnel were talented artists who got the opportunity to show their work at the Lucas Festival of Art in 1974. Among these I recall seeing work by one of our own from Shaftmoor Lane – general foreman Harry Tonks.

A popular pastime at Shaftmoor Lane was chess. There were several so skilled in the art of chess that they gave lessons to novices. Many enjoyable hours were spent watching or taking part in sporting activities like football and cricket at Prospect Lane, Solihull or College Road. Football and cricket were the most popular sports at Prospect Lane and at Moor Lane, but fishing and bowls were the favourites for others. These sports were not just confined to the Birmingham area but throughout Lucas as a whole. Nearly all the factories, shop floors and offices would have inter-factory sports activities and competitions which allowed many to visit and enjoy the facilities of other parts of the company.

Dancing was a popular pastime and several factories ran social events. Lucas had a social club in Soho Hill, Handsworth. The Foreman Recreational Organisation which operated out of many factories organised all types of events, including dances. BW3 used the Springfield Ballroom in Sparkbrook on the Stratford Road, while those at Great King Street used S Block most Friday evenings.

An entertainment facility was built at Shaftmoor Lane which was well used and other factories across the country, such as Liverpool, Cwmbran, Burnley and Sudbury, had social facilities to which interworks visits were arranged and we were invited as guests of honour.

Christmas parties were held for children of Lucas employees and these involved the participation of many good 'aunts' and 'uncles'. For three years I was an 'uncle', responsible for a number of children. It so happened that on one occasion the aging Santa Claus was unable to to perform the high-level jump down a chimney, so a new Santa had to be found quickly. Yes, you've guessed it – I was to become the new Father Christmas for the day and I continued to do so for the next twenty-five years, undertaking death-defying feats that only Len Robinson, an engineer at Shaftmoor Lane, could produce. These ranged from paradiving, driving a team of eight horses pulling a sleigh, and a Tarzan-style entrance. I believe Len was the only man alive who could persuade me to take such risks, but the kids thought it was wonderful.

The late Stan Hood of Shaftmoor Lane was the compère and many a time I found myself suspended from a gantry thirty or forty feet in the air while waiting in an uncomfortable position for Stan's cue to descend.

This was the social hub of the company. It all slowly disappeared, but many happy memories remain.

THE OPENING OF SHAFTMOOR LANE SPORTS PAVILION

doubles and Mrs. Bennett presented the prizes. Each year, Mr. Bennett personally provides the prizes for this tennis tournament. After an interesting match, Miss P. Heaven and Mr. R. G. Hughes beat Miss N Morgan and Mr. E. Duncombe by 6-3, 6-4. Afterwards, the visitors made a tour of inspection of the sports facilities and watched a netball match between the girls of Shaftmoor Lane and old 'F.7'. Mrs. Bennett spoke to several of the girls and congratulated them on their good play.

ON Monday evening, September 4th, Mr. Peter F. Bennett, who was accompanied by Mrs. Bennett, opened the new Sports Pavilion and sports facilities at Shaftmoor Lane.

Mr. and Mrs. Bennett were welcomed by Mr. O. A. Miller, the Shaftmoor Lane Member of the General Management Committee of the Sports Club and declaring the sports facilities open, Mr. Bennett referred to the fact that the tennis courts and netball pitches were of the latest type. The girls of Shaftmoor Lane presented Mrs. Bennett with a bouquet of cream roses, the presentation being made by Miss E. Ryder.

Mr. and Mrs. Bennett afterwards watched the tennis final of the mixed

Top Picture: Mr. and Mrs. Peter F. Bennett watching the play and below:

The Mixed Doubles Tennis Final Contestants (reading left to right):—

E. Duncombe, Miss N. Morgan, Miss P. Heaven and R. G. Hughes.

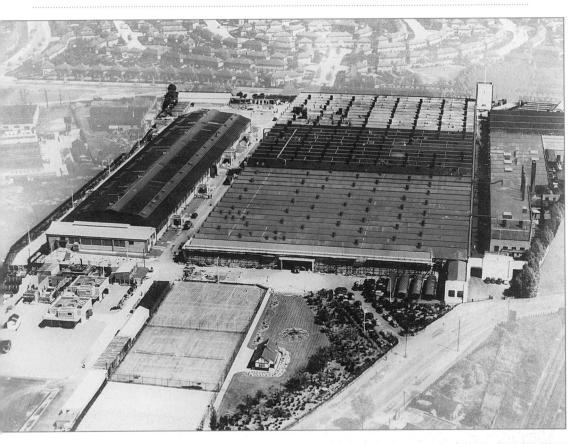

Above: A rare photograph of Lucas Shaftmoor Lane,
1950. The sports area was opened in 1938 by Peter
Bennett but sadly the whole area had been
demolished by 1954.

The Lucas swimming team won the ladies' and men's
invitation team race at a gala in 1938.

This collection of football misfits is about to show them how it's done. The author is third from the right on the front row. I think we lost 5–0.

The winning team in the BW3 darts competition, late 1970s. Factory manager Bernard William (on the right) was no mean darts player himself. The lady players could hold their own versus the men with no problems.

windy day at Burnley Gas Turbine Factory, but this visiting XI don't care. Note the well-pressed trousers Fred Cope, their captain. Back row, left to right: Fred Cope, -?-, Sammy Copp, -?-, -?-, Harold Latham, -?-, ck Gravenor. Front row: -?-, Les Dugmore, -?-, Gordon Cribbins.

knockabout at Prospect Lane. Back row, left to right: Harry Tonks, -?-, -?-, -?-, -?-, Mike Naylor, -?-, -?-, -?-, -, Stan Hood. Front row: Neil Humphries, Ron Moseley, Dennis Coy, Franks Graves, John Brett. Dennis Coy as a dedicated all-round sportsman. His son went on to play professional football for Wolverhampton Vanderers.

A Lucas football team in the 1970s. Gordon Taylor (second from left on the front row) is now the man
responsible for the Football Players' Union.

Bob Butler with his son Neil and test house manager Eric Woolman at the trials of Richard Noble's Thrust
car, Greenham Common, 1980. Richard Noble and his project manager Glynn Bowsher had Joseph Lucas
Aerospace check out some of the car's final systems and also had a tour of the works in that year. As a
thank you they invited these lucky people to see the car's trials.

B.W.3 SENIOR STAFF SOCIAL COUNCIL.
Shalimoor Lae-

11th Annual Dinner
and
Ladies Night

Charter Room
SOLIHULL CIVIC HALL
Saturday, 22nd December, 1979

hree of the managers and their wives at the Ladies Night
nner, held at the Civic Hall in Solihull in 1979. Gordon and
ary Bunce are on the right.

THE WORKS OUTING

The works outing was always the highlight of the year. These were awarded to sections or departments winning one of several categories such as safety, good housekeeping, quality and the like. With the number of factories in the organisation at the time this amounted to a fair number of outings throughout the year. While they were no doubt enjoyable for those participating, they were no less so for those organising them.

I recall as a junior manager my department won such an award, so I gathered up a committee to decide where it was they wanted to go. Their decision was Blackpool. I arranged for the coach to take us and also for the meal when we arrived. Things were going well – too well. We duly arrived at the seaside resort and pulled up thirty yards from the hotel. I got out and made the necessary enquiries with the hotel staff about the meal and returned back to the coach. In the few moments I had gone 170 people had alighted and disappeared. There were now just thirty left. Embarrassed, I tried to explain to the hotel manager what had happened. Alas, he was far from pleased and it did not make matters any easier when the staff roared with laughter at my predicament. They stood idly by while a very irate chef voiced his displeasure.

Those were the days, but my day was not yet over. I finally managed to get most of the people back onto the coach and we proceeded through the illuminations, now minus an odd dozen or so. Many of those who had gone walkabout earlier had been visiting Blackpool's hostelries and were now in dire need of a visit to the loo. Their pleas to stop the coach could be heard as we took our night tour of the lights. . . .

Eventually we arrived home, still minus a dozen or so folk who duly returned days later complaining that we hadn't waited for them. Perhaps the only thing I enjoyed on my day out was to hear the quiet chorus from the back of the coach singing 'Show me the way to go home'.

A good evening out for £2 in 1959.

1938 an outing was arranged for 358 Lucas employees to see the Empire Exhibition at Bellahouston ark, Glasgow. Here they are at breakfast, after which the whole party were left to their own devices.

bove: A party from BW5 on a visit to Burnley for ricket and bowls. It must have been a cold day idging by the long coats.

ight: Harry Tonks at the Lucas Arts Festival held in 974. Harry was the general foreman of the olroom of BW3.

A factory dinner held at the Imperial Hotel, Birmingham, in the 1950s. The hotel was eventually pulled down for new developments in Birmingham in the 1960s. Included in the photograph are Billy Izzard and his wife, Tommy Deathridge and his wife, George and Joan Butler and Harry Walker.

Another group enjoying the celebrations. Included here are Billy Luckman and his wife, Ronnie Laughton and his wife and the author (second from left on the far side).

Fred Cope, Quality Foreman, receiving a cup on behalf of the quality team.

.eft to right: Ron Miles, -?-, Fred Cope, ;ordon Bunce.

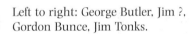

Left to right: George Butler, Jim ?, Gordon Bunce, Jim Tonks.

A social gathering at the Plough, Monkspath, Solihull, *c.* 1957. Left to ight: Jim Grimbley, George Butler, ;ordon Bunce, Bernard Williams, Jack ;ravenor.

Karen Bunce (second from right) at a Lucas children's party in 1968.

A BW5 children's party, 1970. The pirate in the centre is Duncan Butler.

hen Santa's duties were
ished at the Lane he would be
ck on the sleigh to visit Dudley
oad Hospital. Lucas's Santa
und himself extremely popular
r hospital and school
gagements.

'Have you brought some nice
presents for the children, Santa?'
Author Gordon Bunce played the
role of Santa for twenty-five years.

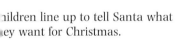

hildren line up to tell Santa what
ey want for Christmas.

Santa with some glamorous helpers.

Susan Butler (left) and Janet Bunce sitting on Santa's lap, Christmas 1961.

hildren enjoying the entertainment at a Lucas children's Christmas party over forty years ago. The two
rls in the foreground of the photograph below (left and centre) are Jacqueline Jones and Susan Butler.

Above: Worthy winners of a competition held at BW3. These ladies from the production department each won £5.

People who worked at the Lucas factories could be described as very giving, not only in money but in their time devoted to worthy causes. BW5 adopted three wards at Dudley Road Hospital and raised well over £60,000 in the 1960s. Shown here are auxiliary nurses from the hospital with the author in 1959.

CHAPTER SIX

Health & Safety

Health and safety have always been a top priority at Lucas. Each and every one of the factories was inspected on a regular basis for any infringement of the company's safety regulations. Annual safety competitions were even held in the factories. This gave employees the opportunity to make suggestions regarding the improvement of safety practices to the management, and the best ideas won prizes. Lucas also cared for the health of its employees, and there was a medical department. This was particularly important because of the use of lead in the factory.

LUCAS SAFETY CAMPAIGN

COMPETITION No. 1

TEST YOUR SAFETY KNOWLEDGE

We publish six pictures with **specially staged faults.**
CAN YOU SEE WHAT'S WRONG?

MARK YOUR ANSWERS :—
Safety Competition,
Personnel Department,
Great King Street, Birmingham, 19.

GIVE YOUR NAME, DEPARTMENT AND CHECK NUMBER.

Answers must reach Great King Street by **mid-day, Monday, November 7th.**

PRIZES :—5/- for the 1st correct answer opened.

2/6 for the 2nd and 3rd correct answers opened.

The Personnel Manager's decision will be final.

SOLUTIONS AND NAMES OF PRIZEWINNERS will be posted up in all main gateways
on Friday, November 11th.

ucas safety campaign competition.

SAFETY COMPETITION
MARKING SHEET

DEPARTMENT .... DATE ....

FOREMAN ....

STATE WHETHER
1st, 2nd or 3rd VISIT ....

Factors taken into consideration:

Age of Department .... Layout of Department .... Processes Involved ....

	Possible Marks	Marks Awarded	Reasons and Remarks
ACCIDENT PREVENTION			
Condition and correct use of: Guards, Fume and Dust Extractors, Hand Tools, Transport and Lifting Tackle ...	15		
Freedom from obstruction of: Gangways, Exits, Fire Appliances, Switchgear and other service points	12		
Standard of stacking and condition of Work, Scrap and Waste Containers ...	15		
Condition of Floors	15		
SAFETY INSTRUCTION			
Safe Working Methods and Correct Dress	9		
Use of Protective Devices and Clothing...	9		
SAFETY RECORD			
Maintenance of Safety Records & Log Book	5		
ALLOWANCE FOR INGENUITY, RESOURCEFULNESS, etc. (Removal of Unsafe Practices)	10		
REPORTABLE ACCIDENT STANDARD	10		

Every department having no reportable accidents during the last twelve months will receive ten marks. Departments not achieving this standard will receive two marks for every reportable accident less than the previous year (with a maximum of ten marks)

TOTAL POSSIBLE MARKS 100

TOTAL MARKS AWARDED ... ...   PENALTY ADJUSTMENT

PENALTY FOR ACCIDENTS

Five marks will be deducted for each reportable accident per 100 employees and pro rata, with a maximum deduction of ten marks per accident.

Signed ....
for Judges

Safety competition marking sheet.
(*People & Productivity, A.B. Waring, 1959*)

Below: Fire and security officers in a training and demonstrations lecture given by Mr H. Guest, Chief Fire Officer, in 1952.

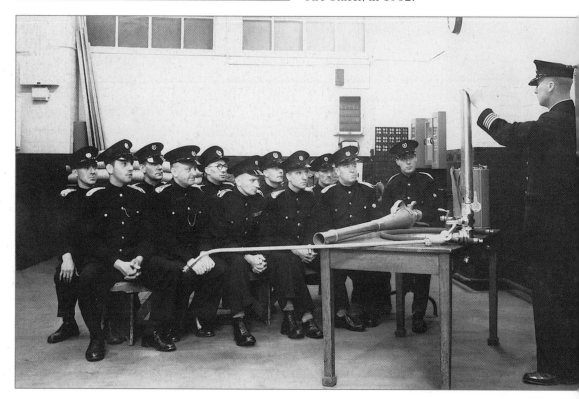

ire and security officers ready to parade outside Great King Street for Her Majesty the Queen's visit in 1955.

A shop-floor display to focus attention on eye safety and protection in Lucas factories. It displays the full range of goggles and visors available to Lucas staff. (*People & Productivity, A.B. Waring, 1959*)

Lucas Workers' Suggestion Scheme poster to promote safety. (*People & Productivity, A.B. Waring, 1959*)

A safe working award being presented to the
Alternator factory in 1985.

Ambulance room, 1930s.

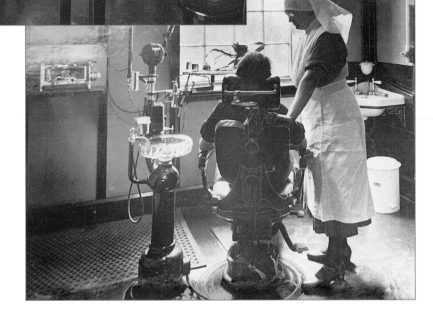

A Lucas medical room in the
1930s.

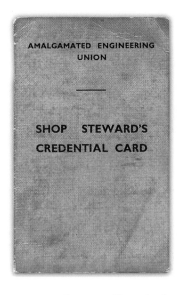

LUCAS UNIONS

Three main unions represented the workers at Lucas: the AEU, the TGWU and another covering those with supervisory posts. All the unions have now amalgamated with others. On balance, the unions were an essential part of daily life at Lucas. There are those who believe that their role was simply to secure improved wage levels, but they did more than this. They alerted people to the dangers of chemicals present in the work place.

Industry has always been hazardous, especially so from the 1960s when many new chemicals and manufacturing processes were introduced. The unions played an important role in this, discussing safety considerations with employers at every stage. Machines had to be guarded and chemical use had to be closely monitored, but despite all the regulations some employees still took shortcuts that endangered their own and their colleagues' lives. Union legislation for improved hours was important. I still recall my working week of 48 hours plus compulsory overtime of 4 hours. Long hours could, and did, lead to accidents.

There are those who will pull things down rather than build, but there is no denying that the great majority of union representatives did a good job, sometimes having to repair fences on both sides, management and shop floor.

Having spent countless hours burning the midnight oil, it is my opinion that strong union representation and informed management generally arrived at common-sense decisions agreeable to both parties.

Many of those elected as union representatives have gone on to positions on councils, responsible for many things which affect the day-to-day running of our cities and towns. Let us not forget that there are those union representatives in Lucas who have been honoured and awarded recognition by both the company and the country.

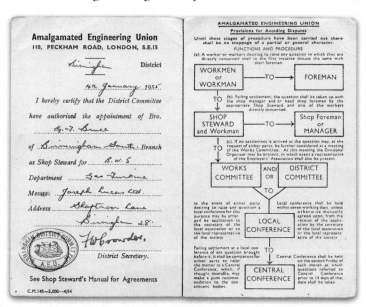

Shop Steward's Credential Card, 1955.

CHAPTER SEVEN
Visits & Presentations

Over the years there have been many official visits to Lucas factories by dignitaries. We have already seen the visits made by Her Majesty the Queen and Harold Wilson in Chapter Three. This chapter features some of the photographs taken on such occasions, along with more informal pictures of presentations to employees.

Norman Crisp, general foreman at BW3, making a presentation in the 1960s.

The Rt Hon. Mr Ron Scannell, Mayor, and his wife visiting Lucas. Ron had been the chief works engineer for the Lucas Electrical Company.

A Lucas party visiting a wire manufacturer in the 1970s.

orman Crisp, the well-respected general foreman, says his goodbyes to the girls (and boys!) at the Lane on is retirement.

urrounded by his fellow managers at BW3 Cyril Jones receives a Teasmade as a leaving present in the 1970s. among those featured in the picture are: Stan Roberts, John Hunt, John Brett, Ken Preece, Ron Moseley, pe ?, Miriam Sands, Joe Farmer, George Wilson, Gordon Bunce, Stan Hood, Bert Onions, Dennis Coy, Albert larke, Mick Cody, Ray Jackson and Neil Humphries. Cyril is flanked by Peter Lea and Edna Poole.

A group of workers from the Marshall Lake Road alternator factory during the 1980s.

ightshift workers at Cranmore Boulevard factory in 1974.

A presentation to ohn Jones at BW5, , 1967. Among hose pictured here re Bob Higgs, ommy Mundy, Eric anner, Maureen eynes, Winnie earns, Ivy Gunnins, ay Madge, Jim onks, Rhoda Hart, ommy Fellows, Jack ravenor, Ron Miles, ob Tuckett, Ray Cox, id Fisher, Les ashford, George utler, Mike Roger, hief quality inspector t BW5.

Farewells to a lovely lady who retired from Marshall Lake Road, *c*. 1984.

A farewell presentation to Roy Barlow, general factory manager, from the staff at Marshall Lake Road, 1984

A retirement presentation to an employee from dynamo winding, 1971. This was clearly close to Christmas as the stage in the background had been decorated. Among those pictured are Ken Frazer, Sheila Walker, Monica Dix, John Hunt and Gordon Bunce.

Production must have stopped altogether during the retirement presentation for Arthur ?, a lovely character from Yoke shop BW3. In the group are Peter Lea (factory manager), Ted Smith (WED general foreman) and John Bott (general foreman of the Yoke shop).

Bernard Williams, factory manager at BW3 starters, making a presentation to George Parker, general foreman short order, in December 1979.

Roy Barlow, general manager at Marshall Lake Road, says his farewells to Dorothy Barnsley, secretary October 1985.

Roy Barlow earlier in his career and Stan Roberts, finance manager, making a retirement presentation to a member of staff at Waverley Works, 1965.

Gordon Bunce and Jack Gravenor (foreman BW5) presenting retirement gifts on behalf of the girls from quality and production, 1959.

A retirement presentation being made to Agnes Scott, 1960s. Also in the photograph are Ann Bridie, Sylvia ?, Billy Glover, Eileen ?, Freddie Simmons and Gordon Bunce.

Lighting design department chief at Cannock, Charles Spencer, and Don Warton are among those present a a leaving presentation in the early 1980s.

The girls of the rotor and winding line at Shaftmoor Lane Dynamo, with 'Little Billy' on the far right of the picture, c. 1968.

orothy Barnsley at
arshall Lake Road in
out 1980.

Gordon Bunce, general foreman, makes a presentation in the late 1960s. Note the proliferation of mini
skirts and bouffant hairstyles in the picture.

Ladies from the miniature (diodes) line at Mere Green, 1976.

A happy group make a presentation in the despatch department of Great Hampton Street, 1961.

leaving do in the mid-1980s at the Mere Green factory. On the far right is Sylvia Warton.

College Road
mployee surrounded
y cards and gifts.

Sylvia Warton's birthday at AB College Road, December 1990.

A colourful retirement send-off for Betty at College Road, 1985.

rnard Bird, superintendent at BW3, with Gordon Bunce, early 1980s. This photograph was taken at the fety awards ceremony.

hese two ladies
ad reached
gnificant
vedding
nniversaries
nd the
ccasion was
narked by their
olleagues at
ucas, 1980s.

Goodbyes are said to the retiring supervisor at BW4, Shaftmoor Lane factory, 1970s.

Lucas employees photographed outside BW4 lamp factory during the 1980s.

Staff from the factory gathered outside Marshall Lake Road in 1984.

upervisors and managers at BW3 say their goodbyes
o a grand foreman, Ernie Laughton, in 1971.
mong those pictured here are Bert Onions, Doug
larke, Neil Humphries, Stan Hood, Ted Smith, Ron
Ioseley, Joe Farmer, Bob Milburn, Gordon Bunce,
eorge Wilson, Ernie Laughton, Dennis Coy, Ron
ughes, Fred Simmons, John Brett and Mick Cody.

ohn Hunt, manager, cutting his farewell cake before
aving to take up a new position as general manager
1 the 1970s. Len Drysdale (left) became general
1anager at Marconi.

THE LUCAS LONG SERVICE CLOCK

Lucas long service clocks were made by the clockmakers F.W. Elliott Ltd in London, founded in 1886. Each clock was handmade by craftsmen with every care taken in its assembly. The casing was made from solid Honduras mahogany and should you notice their guarantee it reads: 'It is most unfortunate but a slight cracking of the veneer may occur after two or three hundred years.' How's that for excellence?

Where did all the years go? Time goes by so quickly and what seems like yesterday is in fact twenty-five years. For those reaching this milestone was the choice of a mantel clock or a gold wristwatch. For those reaching forty years the gift was a silver casket and a cheque.

Eighty-six people made it to forty years service in 1987. They were awarded their long service caskets by Lucas chairman Tony Gill on 5 October that year at Great King Street. In attendance were Dr Alan Watkins of Aerospace and Bob Dale from Lucas Automotive.

All long service personnel on reaching their time would be invited to a chairman's lunch. If you were lucky you might have shared a table with the chairman himself, but at every table would be a director or very senior manager to keep you company. These occasions were as important to the company as to the employees and with so many people reaching long service figures, these events were held on a regular basis.

Presented by the Directors to

GORDON THOMAS BUNCE

*as a mark of
appreciation & goodwill
upon completing*

25 YEARS

loyal & efficient service with

LUCAS

*Chairman
September 1979*

The author, Gordon Bunce and the certificate of his twenty-five year long service, presented in 1979.

Doug Waltham, engineering director, with Ken Bridgewater, factory manager, at a long service gathering at Great King Street, 1980s.

Presented
by the Directors to

Joseph H. W. Clements

as a mark of appreciation &
goodwill upon completing

Twenty=Five Years

Loyal and Efficient Service
with

Joseph Lucas Ltd.

NOVEMBER 1964

The certificate presented to Joseph Clements for twenty-five years long service, 1964.

Jack Bullen and his wife on the occasion of his retirement party in 1985. It has proved impossible for me to identify all those featured in these photographs, but among them are staff from BW5, including Kathy Lowe, Jacky Newman, Bernard Tennant and Steve Nye.

A retirement presentation to Ron Hewett. Left to right are Nigel Stanford, Bob Butler and Ron, December 1987.

Ron Hewett's retirement with a cross-section of staff from the engineering department, December 1987.

ne of the ladies
om planning at
W3 at her
tirement
thering,
980s. Among
ose present are
rian Hubbal
d Mike Naylor.

ob Milburn (factory manager at BW3 Shaftmoor Lane) wishes a happy retirement to Ernie Laughton in
971. In the photograph are Gordon Bunce, Mick Cody, John Bott, Joe Farmer, George Wilson, Ted Smith,
eter Lea, Stan Hood, Dennis Coy, Mick Cody and Ron Moseley.

Managers and senior engineers at BW3 Shaftmoor Lane, 1985. Left to right: Maurice Wells, Tom Gannon, Gordon Bunce, Peter Hopkins, Brian Hubbal.

Frank Graves, former night-shift manager at BW3, is seen here being prepared for his enthronement as Mayor of Appleby-in-Westmorland, Cumbria. He retired there after many years of service at Lucas.

CHAPTER EIGHT
Lucas Advertising

Advertising is an accepted part of everyday life. Lucas spent millions annually bringing to our notice the vast array of goods which are available. Lucas built up a huge aftersales business, supplying some 90 per cent of the British automotive industry, and also set up depots across the country in most large towns and cities.

The Midlands had the Great Hampton Street depot which ran the Lucas sales and service and the well-known B90 exchange system. This was a way of salvaging a worn unit by rebuilding and refitting new parts as required making the component as new but at a fraction of the cost.

A Lucas sales counter in the 1930s. Note the slogans that appear at the top of the picture.

The Lucas depot at Great Hampton Street in 1930.

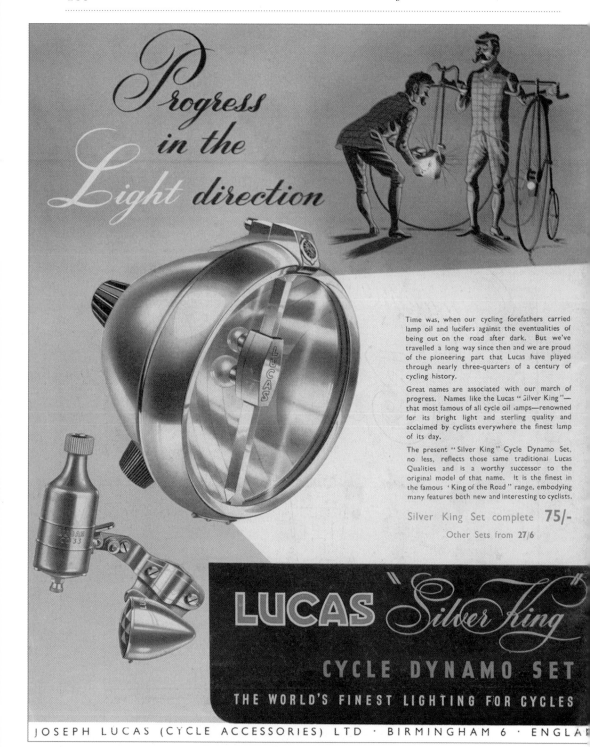

A first-class lamp, but perhaps a bit expensive!

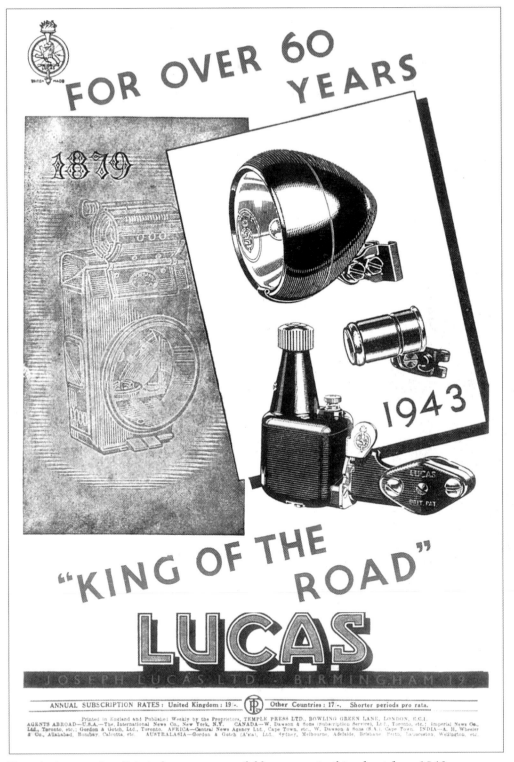

Even during wartime Britain lamps were available, as seen in this advert from 1943.

Lucas fog lamps were adaptable and fitted to many different types of vehicle.

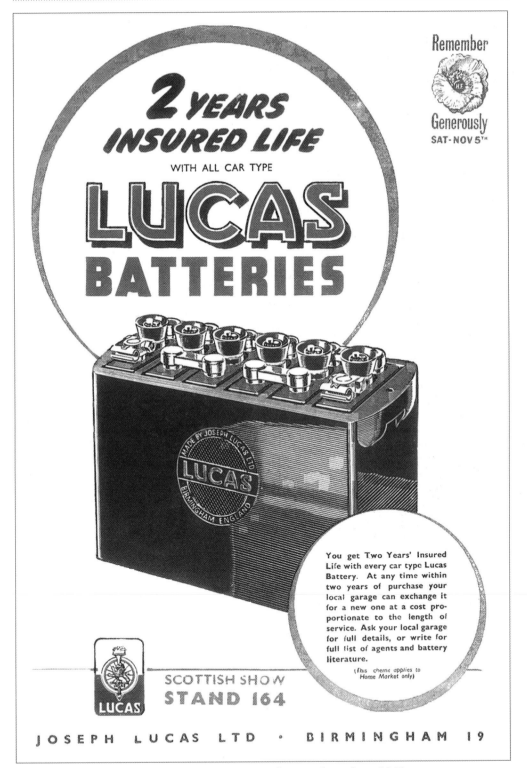

Lucas manufactured a good, serviceable battery. This one dates from 1949.

LUCAS

MANUFACTURERS OF

"KING OF THE ROAD"

ELECTRICAL

EQUIPMENT &

ACCESSORIES

Joseph Lucas manufactured his first lamp in 1878 and called it 'The King of the Road'.

T. B. I. W.

PATENT "KING OF THE ROAD" HUB LAMPS,

WITH ADJUSTABLE BEARINGS AND ARRANGEMENT FOR LIGHTING IN A WIND.

OPENED FOR PUTTING INTO THE WHEEL.

Improved Pattern for 1883.— No. 112B.- For Bicycles.

	Japanned.	Nickeled Tin.	Nickeled Brass.
Size 0, with 3-inch Front Glass	15/-	22/-	29/-
„ 1, „ 3½ „	16/-	23/6	30/6
„ 2, „ 4 „	18/-	27/6	34/6

112T.—For Tricycle axles without Lubricators in the centre, and not requiring Lamps with divided or double barrels, 6d extra to above.

No. 116.

For Tricycle Axles with Lubricators.

	Japanned.	Nickeled Tin.	Nickeled Brass.
Size 0	16/6	23/-	30/-
„ 1	17/6	27/-	33/-

When ordering Tricycle Lamps give the name of the Tricycle they are to fit.

LAST YEAR'S PATTERNS, Nos. 54 AND 57, CAN BE HAD AT SAME PRICES AS BEFORE, OR JAPANNED, 6d. LESS, AND NICKELED, 1/- LESS THAN ABOVE PRICES.

As illustrated in the 1883 catalogue. Although the King of the Road hub-lamp was patented, it was widely copied. This involved Joseph Lucas in a successful action which was published in *The Times* Law Reports

A very early piece of advertising.

Temperature 'below' this morning—touch of the starter, engine leaps into life—always the same, positive result with a Lucas battery. Get a good start today and every day with Lucas!

LUCAS
BATTERY FILLER
Automatically
regulates
topping up
of cells. **6/6** d.

LUCAS
BATTERY MASTER SWITCH
safeguards parked vehicle
and isolates battery
from all
electrical
equipment

27/6 d.

with

LUCAS

FOR CARS
COMMERCIAL VEHICLES
AGRICULTURAL TRACTORS
MOTORCYCLES etc.

BRITAIN'S BEST BATTERY

JOSEPH LUCAS LTD. BIRMINGHAM 19

Printed in England by Bradbury, Agnew & Co. Ltd, at The Bradbury Agnew Press, Saffron Hill, London E.C.1 for The Countryman Ltd, and published quarterly in March, June, September and December at 10 Bouverie Street, London E.C.4
Editorial Office: Burford, Oxford   Tel: Burford 2258   Winter 1961

Lucas marketed its batteries as being the best available in Britain.

A well-known Lucas image. Note the Lucas slogan – 'The King of the Road' – on the signpost in the background.

The B90 unit exchange service was an excellent way of obtaining a first-class unit at a much reduced cost.

TIME SAVED – MONEY SAVED

Electrical breakdown on your tractor can wreck your work plan – if you have to send the unit for repair. Far better 'phone your local Agricultural Engineer who will bring a Lucas B90 Exchange Unit 'off-the-shelf' and fit it on the spot. It keeps the work going and saves you money in the long run. Every B90 unit is rebuilt to the same quality standards as Lucas original equipment and it also has the latest modifications built into it. Guaranteed for 12 months and backed by a Certificate of Warranty, every B90 unit also bears a visible external seal – sign of a genuine unit. Remember – Lucas B90 is the quick, dependable answer.

LUCAS
B90 UNIT EXCHANGE SERVICE

JOSEPH LUCAS LTD · BIRMINGHAM 19

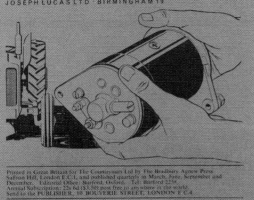

Printed in Great Britain for The Countryman Ltd by The Bradbury Agnew Press Saffron Hill, London E.C.1, and published quarterly in March, June, September and December. Editorial Office: Burford, Oxford. Tel: Burford 125.
Annual Subscription: 22s. 6d. (\$3.50) post free to anywhere in the world. Send to the PUBLISHER, 10 BOUVERIE STREET, LONDON E.C.4.

HOW LUCAS B90 HELPS THE FARMER....

quick answer to electrical breakdown

If a starter, generator, etc., should fail, repairing can mean your tractor (or car) standing idle. Better your local agricultural engineer or garage should replace with a Lucas B90 unit — available off-the-shelf through the local B90 Stockist.

B90 units — Lucas rebuilt to no-compromise standards — are passed only after thorough testing. Each carries an external seal of quality, is backed by 12 month guarantee. Moreover, fixed exchange prices mean you get a more accurate estimate of cost.

LUCAS

LUCAS B90 UNIT EXCHANGE SERVICE
saves time now – and money in the long run
JOSEPH LUCAS LTD · BIRMINGHAM 19

QUALITY ELECTRICAL EQUIPMENT FOR CARS

LUCAS.. the Name that has been associated with the British Motor Industry throughout the reigns of six Sovereigns.

LUCAS

*Pre-eminent in
Design & Performance
for over 80 years*

Lighting, Starting, Ignition, Batteries, Accessories

By appointment to
Her Majesty the Queen
Suppliers of Electrical Equipment
JOSEPH LUCAS LTD

JOSEPH LUCAS LTD · BIRMINGHAM, 19

Super finish and accuracy

No. 2. Precise and immediate control of fuel is achieved by the frictionless design and extreme dimensional accuracy of this amplifier valve for pumps and control units.

FUEL AND COMBUSTION SYSTEMS FOR GAS TURBINE ENGINES **LUCAS**

JOSEPH LUCAS (GAS TURBINE EQUIPMENT) LTD., BIRMINGHAM & BURNLEY

These 1950s/1960s adverts refer to gas turbines. In the 1970s gas turbines became part of the Aerospace division.

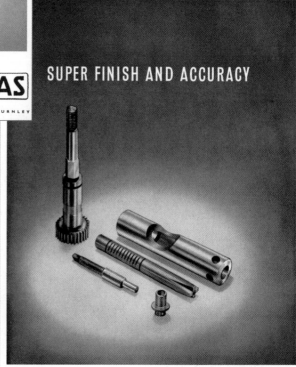

SUPER FINISH AND ACCURACY

No. 1. High pressure fuel flow controlled by low torque manual throttle valve using components of high surface finish with an accuracy of twenty-millionths of an inch.

Fuel and Combustion Systems for Gas Turbine Engines

JOSEPH LUCAS (Gas Turbine Equipment) LTD., BIRMINGHAM & BURNLEY

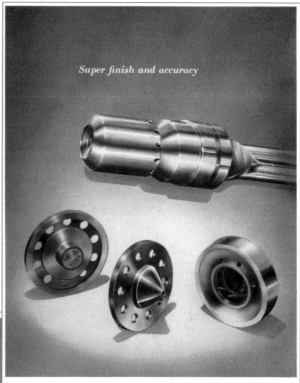

Super finish and accuracy

No. 6. Dimensional accuracy and super finish of burner components ensure efficient fuel atomisation over a wide flow range.

FUEL AND COMBUSTION SYSTEMS FOR GAS TURBINE ENGINES **LUCAS**

JOSEPH LUCAS (GAS TURBINE EQUIPMENT) LTD., BIRMINGHAM & BURNLEY

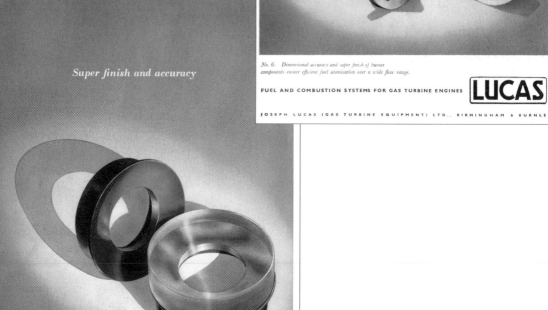

Super finish and accuracy

No. 7. The optical maker's art applied in producing camplates for high-pressure fuel pumps.

FUEL AND COMBUSTION SYSTEMS FOR GAS TURBINE ENGINES

JOSEPH LUCAS (Gas Turbine Equipment) LTD. BIRMINGHAM AND BURNLEY

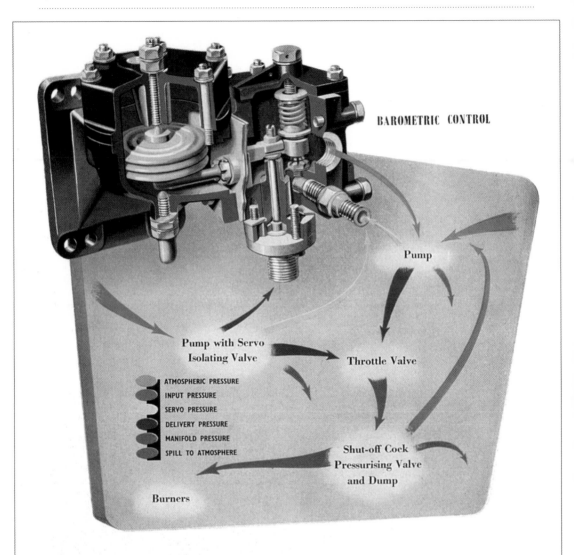

BAROMETRIC CONTROL

Pump

Pump with Servo
Isolating Valve

Throttle Valve

ATMOSPHERIC PRESSURE
INPUT PRESSURE
SERVO PRESSURE
DELIVERY PRESSURE
MANIFOLD PRESSURE
SPILL TO ATMOSPHERE

Shut-off Cock
Pressurising Valve
and Dump

Burners

The LUCAS Barometric Control is a precision instrument

which maintains the correct pump delivery pressure in accordance with variation

in altitude and forward speed.

LUCAS

JOSEPH   LUCAS   (GAS   TURBINE   EQUIPMENT)   LTD: BIRMINGHAM

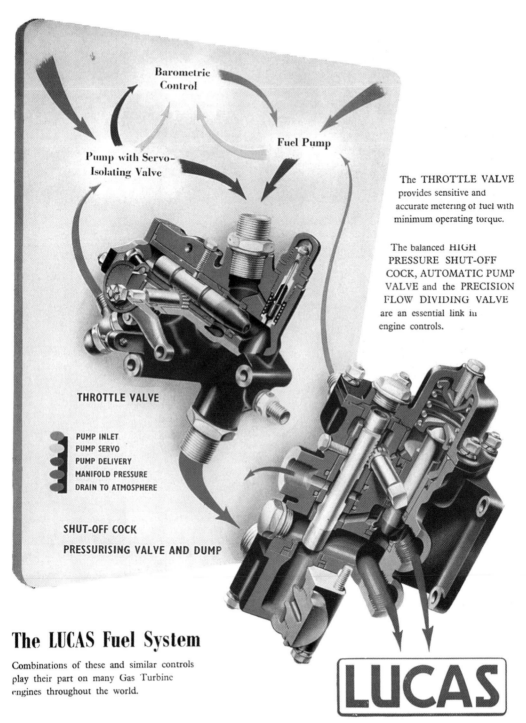

Barometric
Control

Fuel Pump

Pump with Servo-
Isolating Valve

The THROTTLE VALVE
provides sensitive and
accurate metering of fuel with
minimum operating torque.

The balanced HIGH
PRESSURE SHUT-OFF
COCK, AUTOMATIC PUMP
VALVE and the PRECISION
FLOW DIVIDING VALVE
are an essential link in
engine controls.

THROTTLE VALVE

PUMP INLET
PUMP SERVO
PUMP DELIVERY
MANIFOLD PRESSURE
DRAIN TO ATMOSPHERE

SHUT-OFF COCK
PRESSURISING VALVE AND DUMP

The LUCAS Fuel System

Combinations of these and similar controls
play their part on many Gas Turbine
engines throughout the world.

LUCAS

JOSEPH   LUCAS   (GAS   TURBINE   EQUIPMENT)   LTD.   BIRMINGHAM

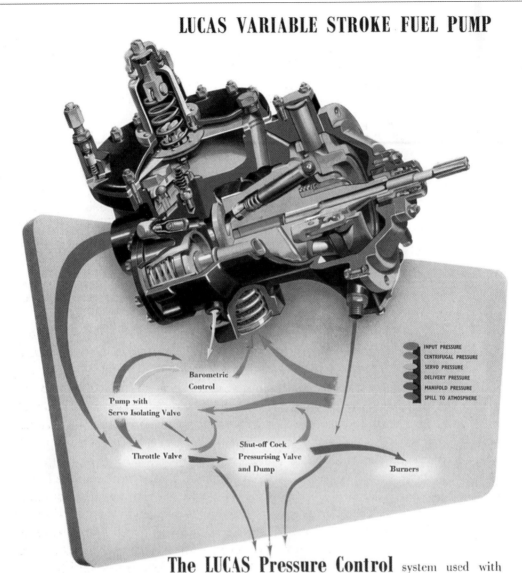

LUCAS VARIABLE STROKE FUEL PUMP

INPUT PRESSURE
CENTRIFUGAL PRESSURE
SERVO PRESSURE
DELIVERY PRESSURE
MANIFOLD PRESSURE
SPILL TO ATMOSPHERE

Barometric Control

Pump with Servo Isolating Valve

Throttle Valve

Shut-off Cock Pressurising Valve and Dump

Burners

The LUCAS Pressure Control system used with this pump on the larger centrifugal type engine is illustrated in schematic form as a complete system.

Lucas pumps were fitted to the first operational jet aircraft in 1942. Today, Lucas fuel pumps and associate equipment are used on gas turbines in most countries of the world.

LUCAS

J O S E P H   L U C A S   (G A S   T U R B I N E   E Q U I P M E N T)   L T D .   B I R M I N G H A M

CHAPTER NINE

End of an Era

The photographs of the demolition of the Lucas factory in Great King Street in this chapter are from Len Wily's collection. Len was an apprentice at Lucas in 1940 and worked in the trade instruction department. He joined the RAF during the Second World War, but returned to Lucas at Shaftmoor Lane in 1947 as an auto fitter dealing with important plant. Some time later he was asked to join the training department to pass on his knowledge to the up-and-coming apprentices. This department at Great Hampton Street was finally moved to College Road and here he worked until his retirement.

Demolition of the Great King Street site took place in 1994–5 and marked a sad end to the imposing factory which had been such a distinctive part of the the Hockley skyline for so many years. Two world wars had failed to put a dent in the factory, but now the contractors' bulldozers succeeded in razing the building to the ground. The once-mighty factory I had gazed up at from the corner of Farm Street and Wheeler Street was no more. All that remains now is the sculpture of the Lucas Lion which now hangs proudly on the gable-end of 36 Wheeler Street, one of seventy-eight houses erected in the area after the demolition of the Lucas factory.

It is sad to think that the Great King Street factory, once the bastion of the Lucas company, has gone. Its demise heralded the end of Lucas. There are still businesses that occupy former Lucas premises, but now they have new names over their doors.

So many people have worked for the Lucas company, many generations of families have come and gone, but alas no more. Perhaps the bricks and mortar have disappeared, but the spirit still remains. Wherever you go you are sure to meet someone who once worked for Lucas, or had a family member who did.

Lucas was once described as being like a huge family. This sums up the feelings of so many who had the privilege of working for the company. Now only memories remain.

The demolition
of Lucas Great
King Street,
1994.

The former restaurant block in Farm Street.

The former laboratory entrance.

Looking up Great King Street from Farm Street.

Part of Great King Street under demolition, 1994. This area used to house the directors' conference facilities, and other rooms and offices.

Acknowledgements

While it is not possible to acknowledge all those who have assisted me in the process of putting together this book, there are some without whose support this book would undoubtedly not have been possible. My special thanks go to:

Rolston Barlow, David Fell, Ronald Hopkins, Edna Pool, Barbara Sabin, Lennard Wily, George Butler, Bob Butler, Roy Middleton, Sylvia Warton, Karen Mawdsley, Jacqueline Hill, Anne Gillette, Tim Crowe, Raymond Saunders, Reg Peach, Peggy Stevens and the late R.H. Lea.

Lucas Great King Street by night.